NLP Techniques

An Introduction to Learning NLP for Beginners

Includes NLP for Careers, Relationships, Confidence, Habits, Fears and Productivity

Sarah Carter

Contents

Foreword

NLP systems are designed to provide for the development of an individual's excellence levels in certain circumstances while also generating the empowering belief of the particular techniques.

In this book, you will learn about the power of NLP and help you achieve a more fulfilling life.

Chapter 1: What is NLP?

Background

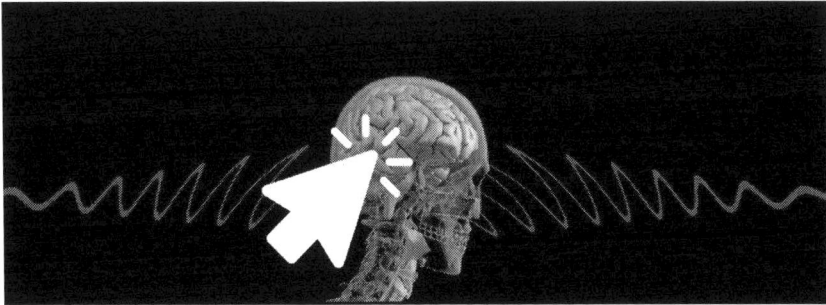

NLP is an abbreviation for Neuro Linguistic Programming. It describes three basic systems within multiple connecting systems. These three systems are the neurology, language, and programming.

Neuro – refers to the neurological system, the way you use senses to translate your experiences into thought processes, both conscious and unconscious.

Linguistic – refers to the way you use language to make sense of your experience and how you communicate that experience to yourself and others.

Programming – is the coding of experience. A program is a series of steps designed to achieve a specific result. The results you achieve and the effects that you create are a consequence of your personal programs.

The Basics

The neurological system regulates the different body functions while the language system determines how the individual communicates and interacts with others.

The programming system determines the kind of world the individual creates based on the neurology and language systems.

The three systems deliver the oneness of mind, language and behavior or interaction. The three systems interact to produce the individual's image of their world.

The NLP processes in a multi-dimensional way to develop flexible behavioral adjustments and competence.

The systems also form strategic, mental and cognitive thinking which derives an individual's behavioral patterns.

The NLP systems also develop an individual's excellence levels and empowering beliefs. It also facilitates self-discovery, exploring the individual's identity and mindset.

NLP also involves spirituality for the individual to understand human existence to a higher level. In essence NLP is not only develops competence and excellence but also the development of wisdom and vision.

Chapter 2: NLP Helps You Grow

Background

NLP helps you grow both mentally and physically in many ways. Initially it may appear quite simple but there are many underlying complications and implications.

Personal Growth

The ability to understand the various levels of both an individual's and other's understanding and thought processes makes it easier to relate to each other and enables more effective communication.

This individual's senses process the information such as sight, smell, touch, hearing and taste. Individuals use these senses and process the information in different ways.

When it comes to communication the senses most used are the sense of sight and hearing.

Correctly identifying the processing used by the receiving individual ensures the information is correctly understood.

It is harder to communicate with other individuals if they use different NLP systems to process information. This may lead to confusion that needs to be addressed.

Identifying the best form of communication for an individual therefore enables quicker and easier transfer of information. If the form that is best suited is visual then perhaps being exposed to a lot of visually presented information would facilitate faster absorption.

If the mode of information is auditory then those that are better able to absorb auditory instructions or information would benefit.

Chapter 3: NLP and your career

Background

There are great benefits in understanding the NLP of those around you. This will enable more effective communication leading to the generation of more benefits.

Your Work

Understanding NLP is very important in the workplace. If the business is using communication methods that are not achieving the desired results, the business should consider alternative communication options.

For example, it would be worthwhile to establish how your manager or supervisor prefers to receive information. This may be different by individual, so you need to establish the preference of each person. Once the preference is established, you should try to use that communication method for that individual as much as possible to achieve the best results, whether it be visual or audio etc.

The same approach can also be used with co-workers to establish their preferred communication method. If the transfer of information is more effective, this can lead to a workforce being more productive and generating higher quality results.

This will lead to a better working environment as people understand the communication methods are being adjusted to reflect their receptiveness.

Once the different information absorption capabilities of individuals is understood, the necessary adjustments should be made to ensure the most effective method is used.

Short courses are available for those interested in adopting the NLP method to advance their careers. These courses normally encourage the participants to understand and refine their own NLP techniques and models. These courses also involve a lot of practical exercises to help practice the new techniques.

Chapter 4: NLP and Relationships

Background

NLP techniques can also be used to establish successful relationships. People are receptive to different forms of NLP to think and experience their surroundings and perceptions. Understanding and using NLP preferences can have a positive impact on an individual's thoughts, behaviors and beliefs.

Relationships

An Individual's mind will receive and process the information received and this determines the individual's reaction. The linguistic skills will provide the communication of the thoughts and response to other individuals, then the programming will determine the appropriate actions and the subsequent consequences.

Therefore, adopting NLP strategies in a relationship can help to prevent negative outcomes.

NLP can help enable individuals to handle disagreements and better understand the reasons for a specific reaction or act. Therefore, the individual consciously approaches disagreements in the most appropriate way to reduce any negative responses.

After practice of using this NLP method to address issues, the individual can influence more positive behavior patterns. With practice, this technique will become an unconscious action and therefore easier to adopt.

Furthermore, adopting this NLP method of communication is often found to reduce stress. The method has also been used to establish new and more innovative ways of building relationships.

As communication is frequently an area of contention in relationships, then trying the NLP technique to learn how to better manage communication in relationships is often considered a worthwhile exercise.

Chapter 5: NLP and confidence

Background

NLP methods can be beneficial to an individual in other areas of life. For example, it can be used to improve an individual's confidence.

Self Assurance

A high level of confidence is certainly desirable for any individual. This can be achieved using the NLP method. With practice, the individual can achieve far more with a higher level of confidence.

An Individual's low level of confidence is often considered as a psychological attribute that has not developed or has been damaged. This can be addressed using the NLP method.

The first step is to accept that improving confidence levels is very achievable. Confidence is a method the limbic system uses so the individual takes what they consider the most appropriate action.

Therefore, using the NLP method to improve communication and the transfer and processing of information is what helps the individual to gain the confidence needed.

If an individual is most receptive to visual then adopting this process can lead to a more confident mindset. This is because the mind has already registered visual as an effective method.

If NLP has established an individual is more receptive to Audio then this media form should be used wherever possible to reinforce the confidence. The greater the exposure to positive communication will encourage the mind to adopt this approach more often.

Chapter 6: NLP and habits

Background

Many Individuals have both good and bad habits. The bad habits are often difficult to break. However, using NLP, the mind can be trained to reject bad habits until they stop.

Removing bad habits

NLP can be used to change the individual's perception of a pleasure derived from a bad habit to an unpleasant experience.

This is achieved by tricking the mind into a new thought process which changes the perception of something so the body will associate the habit will something unpleasant.

The next step should be to create a stronger perception in the mind towards the habit to remove even the slightest temptation to return to the bad habit.

The mind is trained to focus on something else as soon as any reference to the habit occurs. Once the mind is able to do this the habit can be broken.

NLP can also be used to adopting good habits. The mind is trained to identify and apply good habits.

This same method can be adopted. The key is to use the communication method most likely to send the intended message to the brain successfully and effectively.

Adopting this approach will in effect program the neuro patterns which in turn will direct the linguistic and communication elements.

Chapter 7: NLP and fears

Background

There are no physical warning signs of fear; the body has an internal mental alert mechanism that warns something negative or painful is about to occur. Most people struggle to accept that fear is just in the mind.

Concerns

NLP techniques can be used to disassociate unwanted emotional feelings such as fear. The mind is trained to replace these associations with more positive thought patterns.

The first step is to identify what thought process normally generates the feeling of fear.

Once this thought process is recognized in the mind then the mind is retrained to disassociate itself from the fear and replace it with something more positive.

Many people find this an effective to overcome their fears.

Chapter 8: NLP and language

Background

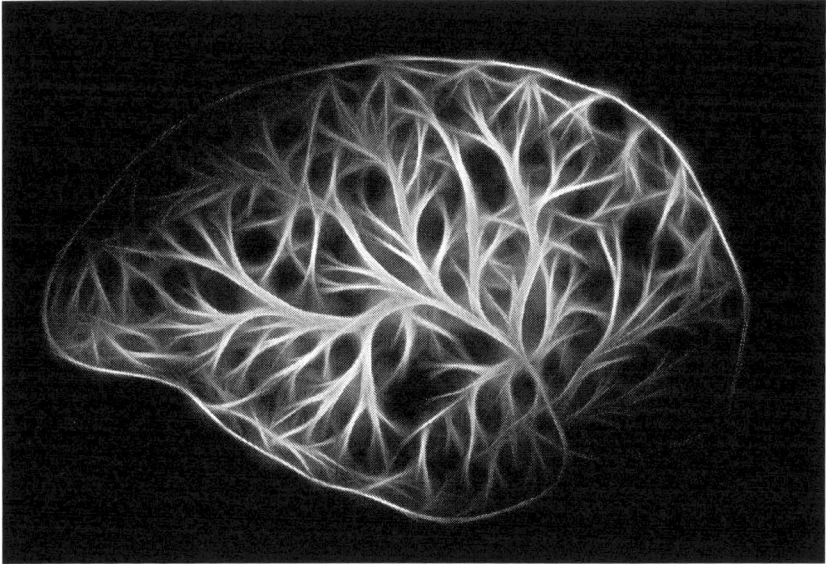

NLP techniques can have benefits when used with language.

This language technique consists of four components

- How senses receive the information
- How the mind processes the information
- How the mind processes outcomes
- The sleight of mouth patterns.

These are proven techniques to influence language and derive the desired outcomes.

NLP and language

The way people speak is often based on the way they think. The way people think is typically based on previous life experiences. Therefore, changing the way people think can influence the way people speak. How the mind reacts to a situation determines the speech patterns used. This then can be changed and even altered through practice.

This technique is often used to influence the tone of voice used when making various statements. Changing the tone with the same words will be projected in a different manner. In addition, the phrasing and structure of the language can also influence the desired outcome.

Conditioning the mind will also influence the outcome. However, this technique is not guaranteed to derive the desired results. This is particularly true if the mind is not yet fully conditioned. Practicing using the NLP method can teach an individual to deliver communication that influences the listener with the desired outcome. This is a very useful tool when conveying information in business situations.

Chapter 9: NLP and productivity

Background

Poor communication can lead to detail being lost or misunderstood which can have an impact on productivity. When this happens the breakdown in communication needs to be addressed. The NLP method can also be used in this situation.

Being more productive

If an individual cannot convince others of their idea or concept this could have a detrimental impact. The impact of not convincing parties of the benefits of the idea or concept could therefore have an impact on productivity.

This could also lead to other negative effects if a problem has not been resolved leading a further decrease in productivity levels.

In this situation, action needs to be taken to improve communication between the parties to improve productivity levels.

The first step is to Identify the behavior having a negative impact on the productivity levels so the issue can be addressed. In addition, the triggers that cause this behavior should also be reviewed.

Therefore, if the individual can influence positive behavior this will have a beneficial impact on productivity levels. Sometimes additional communication may be required to influence the behavior of the recipients and therefore increase productivity.

One NLP technique often used is to address the negative issues is to identify the associated problematic areas and start considering how these issues could be addressed.

By identifying the problematic areas exist also helps acknowledge the issue is not the individual proposing the idea or concept. Once the required changes are implemented the outcome should be better productivity levels.

Chapter 10: Not adjusting your mind

Background

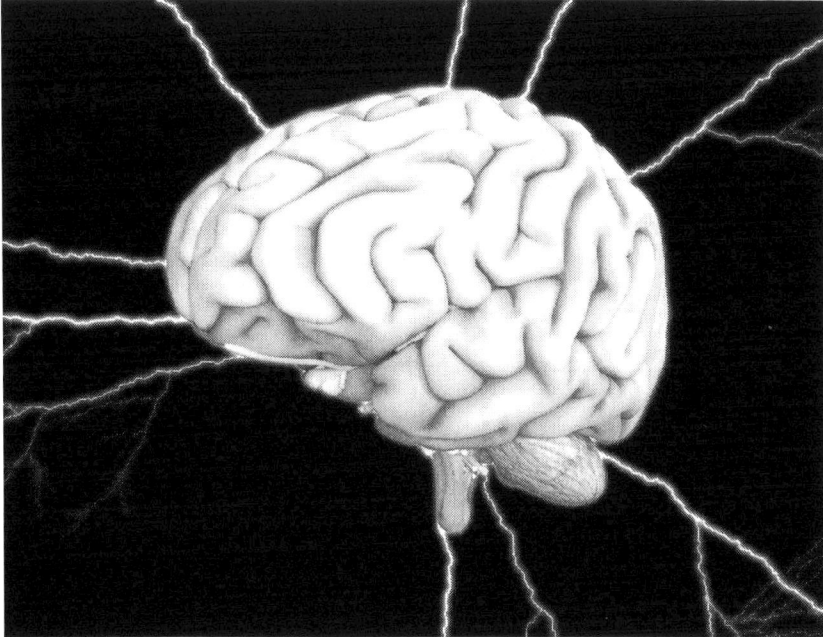

If an individual learns new skills this can create better results, emotions, communication and other positive outcomes and is therefore beneficial. Using the same concept not taking the opportunity to learn and implement the NLP method of making a positive change would be a missed opportunity.

Something to consider

If effort is not applied to improve the way information is accepted and processed by the mind a lot of the potential benefits, such as confidence, can be lost.

Unless you try the NLP method, the opportunity to improve all these areas in life will not be achieved.

These techniques can be applied by any individual in daily life thoughts to improve any positive attributes and also remove any negativity.

The NLP method will help adjust the mind so this will become easier and a more natural process for the individual. The individual will gain confidence, develop public speaking skills and the ability to address negative issues. Furthermore, all this is achieved with a high success rate.

Conclusion

Mastering the brain is an effective way of addressing problems and once mastered there is very little that cannot be achieved.

The hardest part for many people to mastering NLP is fear. The experience of being able to train the mind is phenomenal.

Printed in Great Britain
by Amazon